A Note to Parents

Dorling Kindersley Readers is a compelling new program for beginning readers, designed in conjunction with leading literacy experts, including Dr. Linda Gambrell, President of the National Reading Conference and past board member of the International Reading Association.

Beautiful illustrations and superb full-color photographs combine with engaging, easy-to-read stories to offer a fresh approach to each subject in the series. Each *Dorling Kindersley Reader* is guaranteed to capture a child's interest while developing his or her reading skills, general knowledge, and love of reading.

The four levels of *Dorling Kindersley Readers* are aimed at different reading abilities, enabling you to choose the books that are exactly right for your child:

Level 1 – Beginning to read
Level 2 – Beginning to read alone
Level 3 – Reading alone
Level 4 – Proficient readers

The "normal" age at which a child begins to read can be anywhere from three to eight years old, so these levels are intended only as a general guideline.

No matter which level you select, you can be sure that you are helping your child learn to read, then read to learn!

LONDON, NEW YORK, MUNICH,
MELBOURNE and DELHI

Editor Caroline Bingham
Art Editor Helen Melville
Senior Editor Linda Esposito
Senior Art Editor Diane Thistlethwaite
US Editor Regina Kahney
Cover Designer Giles Powell-Smith
Production Melanie Dowland
Picture Researcher Andrea Sadler
Illustrator Peter Dennis

Reading Consultant
Linda Gambrell, Ph.D.

First American Edition, 2000
4 6 8 10 9 7 5
Published in the United States by DK Publishing, Inc.
375 Hudson Street, New York, New York 10014
A Penguin Company

Copyright © 2000 Dorling Kindersley Limited, London

Published in Great Britain by Dorling Kindersley Limited.

Library of Congress Cataloging-in-Publication Data
Maynard, Christopher.
    Extreme Machines / by Christopher Maynard. -- 1st American ed.
      p.   cm. -- (Dorling Kindersley readers. Level 4)
    Summary: Presents some of the most powerful and unusual vehicles
used today, including the dragster, rocket plane, and stretch limo.
    ISBN 0-7894-5418-1 (hardcover) – ISBN 0-7894-5417-3 (pbk)
    1. Machinery--Juvenile literature. 2. Motor vehicles--Juvenile
literature.
[1. Motor vehicles.] I. Title. II. Series.
TJ147.M34 2000
629.04--dc21   99-043606

Color reproduction by Colourscan, Singapore
Printed and bound in China by L Rex

The publisher would like to thank the following for
their kind permission to reproduce their photographs:
Key: a=above; c=center; b=below; l=left; r=right; t=top
Allsport: Pascal Rondeau: front jacket b, 27br;
Corbis UK Ltd: 34cl; **Frank Spooner Pictures:** Art Seitz 24tl;
Liaison 20b; **Poulet.Ph/Mission** 20clb; **NASA:** front jacket cra,
36-37 b, 40-41, 40cl, 42-43b, 42clb, 43tr, 46bl;
National Motor Museum, Beaulieu: 18tl; **Neill Bruce**
Motoring Photolibrary: Peter Roberts Collection 44b;
Pictures Colour Library: 17cr, 39cr; **Quadrant Picture Library:**
25tr, 26tl, 32-33c, **Rex Features:** Anthony Upton 18-19b;
Pinson 21cr; **The Times:** 24-25 b; **Science Photo Library:**
NASA 42t; **Sporting Pictures (U.K.) Ltd:** 9cr;
Telegraph Colour Library: Planet Earth/Norbert Wu 20tl;
TRH Pictures: front jacket t, 32tl, 37tr, 46t, E. Nevill 47br.

All other images © Dorling Kindersley.
For further information see: www.dkimages.com

see our complete product line at

www.dk.com

Contents

DORLING KINDERSLEY *READERS*

PROFICIENT
4
READERS

EXTREME MACHINES

Written by Christopher Maynard

DK PUBLISHING, INC.

An extreme machine

On land
Endeavor holds the world's land speed record for the fastest truck. In 1993 it zipped along at a staggering 226 mph.

On the sea
Offshore powerboats race along more than three times faster than a car is allowed to travel on the highway.

Most of the cars, boats, and planes we travel in these days are reliable and safe. Most of them are perhaps a little ordinary too, because we see them every day. But there are lots of odd-looking machines that only exist to do something fantastic. They go ridiculously fast or fly incredibly high.

They are extreme machines. Most people would love to have a chance to see them close up or – even better – ride in them.

In this book you'll find out what some of the weirdest machines on earth can do. You'll also find out how they work and how people risk their lives trying to take them to extremes.

In the air
The space shuttle is built to make many trips into space. Its cargo bay is so big it could hold a small whale.

Ray power
Solar cars are powered by the Sun's rays, not by gasoline. This car, the Mad Dog, can reach more than 40 mph (but not on cloudy days!).

Drag-car racing

No tread
Slick tires have no treads, or grooves. Treads in car tires let rainwater out so the car doesn't skid.

The two drivers sat in their drag cars waiting for the next quarter-mile race. They watched an assistant splash water over both sets of rear tires, or slicks. The fat slicks were now slippery as the drivers locked their front brakes and revved their gleaming engines. With a roar that set the packed stadium cheering, the slicks began to spin. Clouds of smoke rose behind the drag cars.

In seconds the rubber slicks turned soft with heat. It gave them a grip on the track that was as sticky as a leech's. There would be no unwanted wheel spin and wasted seconds when the race began, no matter how fast the drivers set off.

Each driver now popped his gear stick into first and gripped the handbrake to hold his car back. Each man felt the engines begin to tug. Before them was a "Christmas tree" of lights, stacked one above another on a pole. The cars were ready to spring forward the instant the lights changed.

Best ever
The fastest recorded drag car took only 5.63 seconds over a quarter-mile track. That's six times faster than a racehorse!

Slow car?
A Ferrari can reach 60 mph in about five seconds. Drag racers do it in just two!

Safety first
A drag car driver wears a fireproof suit, a crash helmet, and a neck brace to help prevent injury.

One of the Christmas tree's lights winked on, then another. A third flashed green and the two cars rocketed forward. Blink and you would miss the race! Less than eight seconds later the cars screamed past the finish line a quarter of a mile down the track. Having reached 150 mph, they were traveling well over twice as fast as a car on a highway.

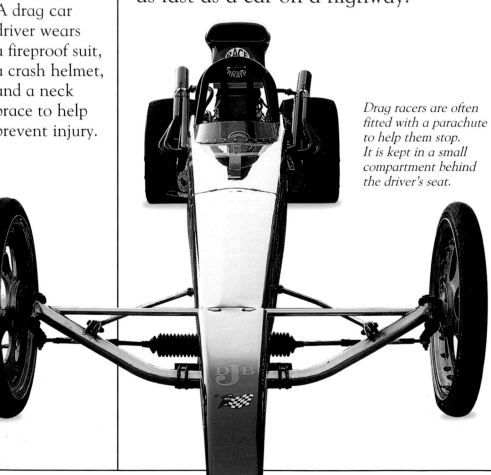

Drag racers are often fitted with a parachute to help them stop. It is kept in a small compartment behind the driver's seat.

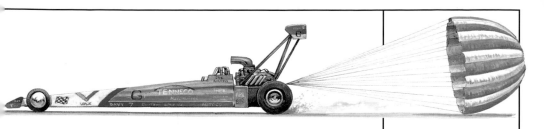

The drivers released parachutes to help slow the cars. The race was so close that it was hard for the excited crowd to see which car had come in first. Fortunately, the electronic timer caught it all. The winner, in the left-hand lane, was seven-hundredths of a second faster!

The drivers steered over to the road that led the loser from the racing lanes and the winner to his next race. Both drivers were handed a small ticket that noted the time of their run and their final speed.

For the rest of the day, the winning car beat every competitor it met. After two hours, the driver had won seven races. He had been racing for less than a minute in all.

Not so quick
Drag bikes are slower than drag cars. They have to be to avoid rearing up and doing wheelies. That would slow them down even more!

Slower still
Drag trucks are even slower than drag bikes. Because of their size, they take twice as long as a drag car to tear down a quarter-mile strip.

9

Getting dizzy
Le Mans cars follow a circuit that is about eight miles long. They'll lap the circuit some 350 times during the race.

Running start
Drivers used to start Le Mans by running across the track and jumping into their cars. This no longer happens because it is very dangerous.

Le Mans

One of the world's most famous endurance races is held every year close to Le Mans, a town in France.

The town comes alive each May and June when dozens of powerful cars and thousands of excited spectators arrive. The cars have come to take part in a grueling 24-hour-long race around a long circuit near the town. It's fast, it's tiring, and it's thrilling!

In fact, although they only drive around an eight-mile circuit, by the end of Le Mans the cars have covered almost 3,000 miles. It's the same as crossing the U.S. once – and then coming more than a third of the way back!

Wet or dry?
Grooved tires are used if it rains, smooth slicks if it's dry.

On the day of the race, 70 to 80 cars pull away from the starting line. It's an incredible sight. Round and round the cars roar, circling the course in the time it takes to soft-boil an egg. Each car has a team of three drivers who change places after 15 circuits. That's just over an hour of driving each time.

Used once
Windshields usually last one race only: they are badly damaged in the 24 hours.

The drivers need to stay as fresh as possible. If they get tired, it's easy to crash. That's why all Le Mans cars must have a towing eye on the front and back. The eye is used to tow them off the track if they crash.

Low = fast
Le Mans cars are low, at just over three feet high, and wide. This helps them to hug the track, even at high speeds.

Quick change
A Le Mans car can be jacked up in seconds, raising the car six inches. Each wheel is held on with just one nut. Tires are changed in the time it takes to tie a shoelace.

Who's that?
Racing machines always have numbers so they can be easily identified.

The best place to watch Le Mans is from the grandstands close to the pits – the areas where the cars are serviced. Cars regularly limp into the pits, thirsty for fuel and urgently needing a new set of tires.

Mechanics swarm around a car like bees the moment it rolls to a stop. Each mechanic has a small task that has been repeatedly rehearsed. Within seconds the car is refueled, fitted with fresh tires, and speeding away.

AVANTI 3

Tough truck
This truck competed in an endurance race called the Baja 1000. It covers 620 miles (1,000 km) in Mexico, over rocky and sandy ground.

The pits are busy, not only with cars, resting drivers, and mechanics, but also with photographers and reporters. Behind the pits, each team has a huge garage with mountains of spare parts for the cars.

Drivers have to be careful when they leave the pits. Cold tires don't grip as well as hot, and the cars may skid if they pull away too fast. It's a tricky race. That's why, in 1998, of the 73 cars that left the starting line only 23 managed to finish.

Engine power
Le Mans cars are fitted with engines that have four times the muscle of ordinary cars! Most engines are positioned behind the driver – not in front as in a family car.

13

Thrust SSC

Thrust SSC (the initials stand for SuperSonic Car) was built to take the world land speed record. It was also the first car to go supersonic, or faster than the speed of sound (sound travels at about 760 mph). But the team of people who built the car almost didn't make an attempt at the speed record.

The car was built in Britain but it needed a long, flat stretch of ground to attempt a speed trial. Nowhere in Britain was suitable.

Fast track
Thrust SSC is designed to cut through the air as neatly as possible. It is long, thin, and hugs the ground. This aerodynamic shape helps it to go faster.

However, Black Rock Desert in Nevada was ideal. The desert is long and its surface is smooth. The problem was that the team couldn't afford to buy fuel for the airplane they needed to fly the car over.

Then someone suggested they ask people to donate money to buy 25-gallon amounts of jet fuel. After an appeal on the Internet and publicity in newspapers, money began to pour in. The team soon had what they needed. They were set to go for the record.

15

A speedy truck?
Endeavor holds
the truck land
speed record.
Thrust SSC
is still more
than three
times faster!

A speedy car?
The Maclaren
F1, the fastest
street-legal car
in the world,
can get up to
230 mph.
That's less than
a third as fast
as the SSC.

October 15, 1997, was a perfect
autumn day. It was perfect weather
too for trying to set a new speed
record. As Andy Green, driver of the
SSC, eased open the throttle, the
giant black car began to roll.
It moved slowly at first so its jets
didn't inhale desert dust. As it picked
up speed, the afterburners began to
blaze and poke their 40-foot-long
tongues of flame out behind the
engines. It was an amazing sight.

The driver sat so low he could
only see two miles ahead. To keep on
course he followed a white line of
gypsum powder the team had
sprinkled on the desert floor.

Half way along the track was the measured mile. By the time the car got there it was traveling at 763 mph. That's slightly faster than the speed of sound. It zipped through the mile in under five seconds.

Onlookers saw the 10-ton jet car slip past as steady as a locomotive on rails, chased by a 300-foot-wide carpet of desert dust lifted by the trailing shock wave. A few seconds later the double crack of Thrust's two jet engines breaking the sound barrier split the air.

Two minutes after it set off, the car came to a stop. It was 13 miles from where it started. Thrust SSC was the proud owner of a new world record.

A speedy plane?
A 747 crew, flying overhead at the right moment, would have been shocked to see Thrust SSC moving 180 mph faster than it was flying.

Catching up
Thrust SSC broke the sound barrier on the ground exactly 50 years after the first plane, the X-1, did so in the air.

What about people?
The fastest person in the world runs 100 yards in just under 10 seconds. That's about 24 mph.

Think tiny
Enlarged here, the world's tiniest car is the size of a match head. It is a working model of a 1936 Toyota – but it's 1,000 times smaller.

Think bigger
One of the smallest cars you may spot is the Smart from Daimler Benz. Two will fit into a normal-sized parking space.

Stretch limousine

The first thing the lottery winner did with his prize was to buy the best Cadillac he could. Then he told friends he was going to cut it in half. He wanted a stretch limousine – and that is how they are made!

The car was sent to a special limo-building factory. The owner asked for a "120-inch super stretch limo." That meant the factory would open the car up and lengthen the body by 120 inches, or 10 feet.

The cutters sliced the car as easily as a knife cuts into butter. In went long steel rails and new side panels. Then the car's interior was designed.

A partition separated the chauffeur (show-FUR) and passenger compartments. It had an electric window that slid up and down. Big, soft leather seats were also fitted. Ten people could now sit in the car. With a refrigerator, phone, TV, and VCR, the finished interior looked nothing like a normal car.

With a short stretch of the imagination, it reminded the owner of a luxurious yacht. But instead of a hull it had wheels!

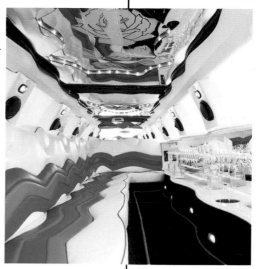

All jazzed up
Limousines are usually luxuriously fitted inside. Neon lights and painted ceilings add to the glamor.

How long?
You could park six large family cars alongside the world's longest stretch limousine.

Deep-sea submersible

Two scientists and a pilot climbed down into Alvin, a deep-sea submersible. The hatches clanged shut. Then a crane lifted the little craft over the ship's side and gently set it down on the waves.

Getting dark
There is no light 3,000 feet below sea level. Submersibles depend on powerful lights if they are going deeper.

Going down
Scuba divers can only dive to 160 feet before the pressure stops them. In an atmospheric diving suit, a diver can go to ten times that depth.

Once in the water, Alvin is stable enough for a person to stand on its top.

The 22-foot-long diving vessel bobbed on the swell and then dipped underwater. Now it moved more like a spaceship than a sea-going ship as it gracefully began to sink. Its journey would take it down almost 2.5 miles into the inky black ocean depths. The descent would take just over two hours.

Alvin's crew was glad to be wearing thermal underwear and heavy sweaters. The water outside was icy cold and that affected the temperature inside. As they huddled in the tiny cabin, only one light was kept on to save power. It was eerily quiet, though the crew did keep in regular contact with the ship above through a cordless telephone.

As it neared the sea floor, Alvin halted and the pilot flipped on a bank of powerful lights. The crew peered out of Alvin's portholes. What would they see?

Going deeper
In the deepest parts of the sea, water pressure is 1,000 times greater than at the surface. Normal submarines cannot go this deep – the pressure would flatten them.

Deeper still
In 1966, a submersible called the Trieste set a world record by diving to more than 36,000 feet.

Staying down
Alvin can stay under water up to 72 hours in an emergency.

Deep thoughts
Alvin can dive deeper than a whale. Trieste goes deeper still.

Skyscrapers of black rock loomed out of the dark. Nearby were the smoking hot-water vents the scientists had come to study. Heated by volcanic rocks deep in the earth, water gushed out of the vents at temperatures hot enough to melt lead. Yet small plants and animals lived around the vents. The scientists hoped to learn more about their lives.

The pilot brought Alvin closer. The machine's big robotic claw swung down to collect samples of the gushing water. The scientists knew this would stink like rotten eggs. Then Alvin moved away to settle on the seabed where the scientists could gather further samples.

After four hours, the work was complete. The pilot released metal pellets from a tank to lighten Alvin's load and the craft began the long two-hour journey back to the surface. It had been a fascinating trip.

Offshore powerboats

What's that?
This odd-looking racing machine is a swamp buggy. It is raced through muddy swamps in Florida. Swamp buggies were originally built as hunting machines.

Each year from June to November, powerboat crews from all over Europe and the Middle East gather for a season of races. In open seas they battle to win the World Championships of offshore powerboat racing.

Offshore powerboats are huge. They weigh the same as five family cars and stretch a good 43 feet. Their massive twin hulls, called catamarans, are made out of two space-age materials – carbon fiber and Kevlar.

The combination is lighter than steel but a lot tougher. Into the hulls go two fighter-plane cockpits – one for the driver and one for the throttleman.

The two crew members are strapped into their seats for safety. Both wear life jackets and crash helmets and each has an air supply. They talk to each other, and to team members on shore, through intercoms in their helmets.

The intercoms are vital pieces of equipment. Once a race begins, the roar of the engines means the crew cannot hear each other without them.

Skirted boats
Tiny hovercraft race at 85 mph every year at World Championships in France. They follow a water-and-wet-grass circuit.

One or two?
Offshore powerboats used to have single hulls and open cockpits. Today's twin-hulled boats, with their closed canopies, are much safer.

Thin and fast
Cigarette boats have won more races than any other boats. They have twin 500-horsepower engines. They were originally used to smuggle cigarettes between the Bahamas and Florida.

Boats jostle for position when a race begins, narrowly avoiding hitting each other. The race course is marked with anchored floats called buoys. The boats have to maneuver around them.

Inside each boat the driver begins checking the navigation system and compass to stay on course. The throttleman watches the wind and waves, trying to guess what the boat will do next.

Running into the wind can speed a boat up, as it lifts the hull out of the water. However, if the boat rises off the top of a wave to fly through the air, the throttle is hauled back. This stops the propeller from spinning too fast and breaking!

The throttleman's constant adjustments can mean the extra mile per hour that will win the race. But at speeds of 150 mph, his moves have to be instant!

Slow down!
Choppy seas can slow a powerboat by 50 mph or more.

Jet boats
In New Zealand, small jet boats are raced up shallow rivers. They have no propeller to catch on the bottom.

Formula 1 boats
These racing boats are fast and furious. They seat one person, and, like offshore powerboats, are twin-hulled. They can speed up from 0 to 100 mph in five seconds.

Hydroplane racing

Speed record
The Spirit of Australia was a hydroplane driven by Ken Warby. In 1978 it set a world record on water of 317 mph.

Hydroplane racing is the fastest and most dangerous of all watersports. On a 2.5-mile course, the best machines shoot down the straight stretches at 200 mph and take corners at 160 mph. It's thrilling to watch these boats in action.

The hulls barely touch the water. Hydroplanes basically travel on a cushion of air. But the boats shake violently, pounding over the surface of the water like hammers.

Bottled air
Hydroplane drivers carry 45 minutes' worth of oxygen in case they capsize.

The violent motion can temporarily blur the driver's eyesight! Yet over a 20-minute race, drivers must tweak the controls to keep their boat as high out of the water as possible. At the same time they try to overtake other hydroplanes. That's not as easy as it sounds.

A boat that overtakes must not cut in front of the other boat until it is more than five boat-lengths ahead. That's because each boat creates a huge "rooster"-tail of spray that flings a ton of water into the air. If this pelted down in the path of a following boat, it would flood the cushion of air the boat was riding on. When this happens, it forces the following boat up and over in a spectacular somersault.

Power crazy
A hydroplane is ridiculously powerful. Its engine is actually four times more powerful than a Formula 1 car engine.

No protection
Hydroplanes used to have open cockpits. But increasing speeds led to more accidents and today's drivers sit in sealed cockpits.

A way out
Hydroplanes are fitted with two escape hatches. One is in the front, and one is underneath the boat, located in the hull.

Speed king
Hydroplanes, like drag cars, can race over quarter-mile lengths. The Spirit of Texas set a quarter-mile record of 5.5 seconds.

A hydroplane is cleverly designed, with a double front hull but a single rear hull. As it picks up speed its two front hulls become airborne.
This means it doesn't have a huge weight of water to move aside.
With only the back hull and propeller dragging in the water, most of its power turns straight into speed.

The secret of hydroplane racing, though, is what the boats use to push themselves along with. They are fitted with a giant helicopter engine.

The engine is fine-tuned to produce an incredible 4,200 horsepower. That's enough power to run 42 good-sized family cars!

The engines do their job, but the speed puts lives in danger. In the past, hydroplaning has killed many drivers. That's why today's drivers sit cocooned in a sealed cockpit fitted with escape hatches and an oxygen supply. Accidents still happen with these speed monsters, but nowadays drivers usually survive.

Strange brew
Many hydroplane engines run on alcohol, gas, or other strange brews of fuel. These give more power than the gasoline used in cars.

Mi-26 helicopter

Next in line
After the Mi-26, the next biggest helicopter is the Chinook. Its freight hold is a third as big as the Mi-26's.

Smallest of all
There's only room for one in the world's smallest helicopter. In fact it only weighs as much as a small adult.

The twin engines coughed and belched smoke as one of the world's largest helicopters, Russia's Mi-26, started up. The noise was tremendous.

Moments later, the helicopter's eight rotor blades began to whisk the air, stirring up the dust beneath. They gathered speed and merged into a whirring disk that was wide enough to park ten lanes of cars beneath it.

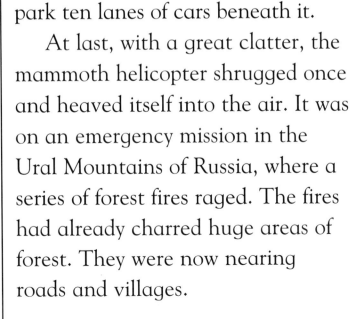

At last, with a great clatter, the mammoth helicopter shrugged once and heaved itself into the air. It was on an emergency mission in the Ural Mountains of Russia, where a series of forest fires raged. The fires had already charred huge areas of forest. They were now nearing roads and villages.

The five-man crew of the Mi-26 had scrambled into the air minutes after the call came through. Their job was to ferry firefighters to the scene of the blaze.

That's why 78 firefighters were now crammed together on the helicopter's cargo deck. Each was fitted out with a parachute and a large pack of firefighting equipment. They were ready for the drop and the task ahead of them.

60 years ago
In 1939, a Russian engineer named Sikorsky, living in the U.S., built the first working single-rotor helicopter.

1,500 years ago
The idea behind a helicopter is more than 1,500 years old. Back then, the Chinese had a toy called a flying top that used feathered rotors to fly.

Back and forth
A helicopter's rotor blades tilt in two directions so a helicopter can fly forward and backward.

As they reached the fires, the helicopter crew could see a wall of smoke. They could not see through it, but several miles west of the smoke line the pilot spotted a winding logging road. This was their drop zone. The tree-lined road was too narrow to set the Mi-26 down, so the pilot hovered at about 1,500 feet while the crew lowered the cargo deck's rear hatch.

In waves, the firefighters dived head-long out of the helicopter. Parachutes snapped open and they drifted down onto the road. Ten minutes later, all 78 men were safely on the ground and the crew was raising the hatch.

The giant helicopter dipped its nose and headed back to base to collect more firefighters.

The X-15

The giant B-52 bomber rumbled down the runway and lifted off. It carried no bombs. Instead a small black dart was tucked under its right wing like a rolled-up newspaper.

The dart was an X-15, a U.S. Air Force experiment to see if it was possible to fly an occupied plane into space. By hitching a ride on the B-52, the X-15 halved the fuel it needed to get airborne. It carried one pilot and was basically a flying fuel tank. It had stubby wings on the side and a rocket engine on its back.

The X-15 was the fifteenth in a line of experimental aircraft that began with the X-1.

The original goal of these planes was to go higher than 19 miles and faster than three times the speed of sound. The X-15 achieved this, and more. It was the first plane ever to fly into space. And it broke all records for being the highest, fastest, and most dangerous way to fly.

Suddenly the X-15 left the B-52. Its engine fired and it climbed straight up as if aiming to punch a hole in the sky. By the time it reached 37 miles there was so little air left that its wings had nothing to bite into anymore.

X-1
The X-1 was the first plane to fly faster than the speed of sound.

Wrong engine
If the X-15 had been fitted with a jet engine, it would have spluttered and died long before reaching space. A jet engine needs air, and there is no air in space.

The X-15 had skids instead of rear wheels.

It now used a dozen tiny rockets to steer itself. Up and up it climbed. By the time it was out of fuel it was over 67 miles up. The pilot could see the curve of the planet and look down on the atmosphere he had left behind.

There is no clear line where atmosphere ends and space begins. Most people in space exploration agree that it happens at about 50 miles up. That's why this pilot, and half his colleagues, earned themselves the right to wear astronaut wings. For at the top of its flight the X-15 was traveling like a spaceship.

Low fliers
High-flying passenger jets cruise around the world at a height of about 7.5 miles. Compared to this the X-15 went nine times higher.

By now the X-15 was rocketing along at about 4,500 mph. That's just over six times the speed of sound. At normal highway speeds, a car would have to travel non-stop for three days and nights to go as far as the X-15 would have done had it kept this up for an hour.

Turning back to Earth, the plane glided down. It was a strange sight. To save weight, it had no rear wheels, only a pair of metal skids – a bit like gigantic skis. After landing, it simply skied along the ground until it stopped. The flight had taken just over ten minutes.

Hot stuff
At six times the speed of sound, the X-15's skin got very hot, reaching a scorching 1,202°F. It had a special metal surface to withstand this.

Getting bigger
Even slower planes, like the Concorde, heat up in supersonic flight. Heat makes metal expand. The Concorde's body swells eight inches in flight.

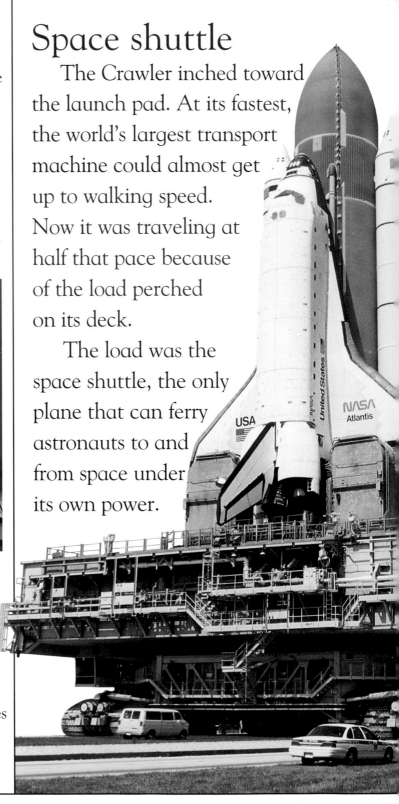

Space shuttle

The Crawler inched toward the launch pad. At its fastest, the world's largest transport machine could almost get up to walking speed. Now it was traveling at half that pace because of the load perched on its deck.

The load was the space shuttle, the only plane that can ferry astronauts to and from space under its own power.

Earlier trips
Before the space shuttle, astronauts were sent into space in rockets. The giant Saturn V rockets were the largest and the most powerful launchers built.

Saturn V

Speed record
In orbit the shuttle flies 30 times faster than a jumbo jet. It would take ten minutes to fly from Los Angeles to New York.

The shuttle consists of an orbiter, which carries a crew of seven astronauts, a giant fuel tank, and two skinny booster rockets. On this trip, the orbiter also carried a satellite to launch in space.

Six hours later, countdown reached zero. With a roar and a blinding glare, the shuttle shot up. Two minutes later, the now empty booster rockets broke free. The main engines thundered on, draining the fuel tank at a speed that would empty a swimming pool in under ten seconds. The emptied fuel tank soon dropped away and the orbiter glided gently into its path around Earth. The seven astronauts were 190 miles up.

Empties
When empty, the two booster rockets drop back to Earth. They are collected to be used again.

41

A long reach
The shuttle's robotic arm is as long as four cars parked bumper to bumper.

In space the astronauts and their equipment became weightless. It was fun, but they had a lot of work to do if they were to launch the satellite.

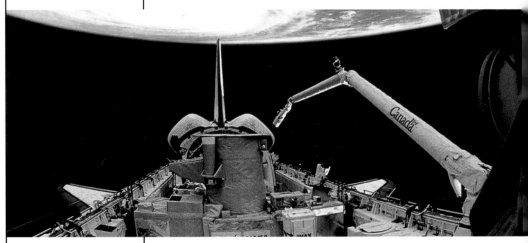

Space chair
Astronauts use a rocket-propelled "armchair" when they work away from the shuttle.

Two astronauts climbed into their spacesuits and entered the orbiter's whale-sized cargo bay. The enormous cargo bay doors swung open. The astronauts then used a long robotic arm to begin the process of launching the satellite.

Checking and launching the satellite took seven days.

Then it was time to return to Earth. Strapped back into their seats, the astronauts heard the puff of the steering rockets. Then the main engine fired. Its power would take the craft out of orbit and return it to Earth.

When the orbiter hit Earth's atmosphere it started to buck and plunge. Meanwhile, the craft blazed red with the heat of plunging through the air at thousands of miles an hour. Special ceramic tiles stopped it from melting.

The orbiter no longer needed its engines. It returned to Earth as a glider, making a neat runway landing.

Space station
Countries with space programs are planning a jointly run station in Earth's orbit. Its permanent crew will show that humans can live in space.

Life on board
In space, the orbiter's seven crew members live in a section at the front of the shuttle. The rest of the craft is a cargo bay – and the massive engines.

Ideas for the future

Ideas for machines of the future may sound odd. But imagine how weird a space shuttle would have seemed to people one hundred years ago.

The Cadillac Evoq is a luxury sports car of the future. If you are ever offered a ride in one, don't reach for the door handles. There are none – the car opens by remote control!

The car can also "see" in the dark. A camera picks up the body heat of people and animals well beyond the beam of the headlights. Their image appears on the windshield, warning drivers to steer clear.

No fuel tank!
People who make new machines try to look for ways to save power. This solar-powered car runs on energy from the Sun.

Speak to me
The Evoq has an on-board, voice-controlled computer. It helps the driver to travel safely.

The car can detect anything behind it in the same way. The Evoq is an intelligent car.

On water, the little Flarecraft L-325 is a boat dressed up like a plane. Known as a wingship, it has a pair of stubby wings, an airplane's tail, and a small propeller above the roof.

As the 31-foot-long craft speeds up, its wings create a cushion of high-pressure air on the water's surface. The cushion is strong enough to lift the five-passenger wingship into the air, where it speeds along at 75 mph. It's much faster than a boat because the water isn't dragging it back. Yet it can't climb more than the height of a grown-up.

That's why the wingship will never be anything but a "boat." The moment it tries to fly higher, the air cushion vanishes and the craft splashes down.

Water flight
As the Flarecraft® speeds up, it rises in the water. At 50 mph, it takes off and cruises just above the surface.

What's that?
This design for a car shows how unusual some ideas for ncw machines can look. It's called the Slug.

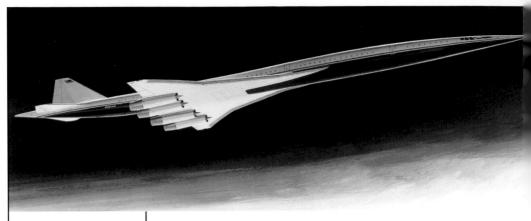

Speed monsters
Supersonic planes of the future will be more than twice as long as the Concorde!

Space rescue
This is a suggested rescue craft for ferrying people back from an international space station if it should ever be needed.

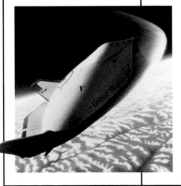

There are exciting plans for future air travel as well. Designers are hard at work on a 300-seat jet airplane that flies at 1,500 mph. That's over twice the speed of sound! The plane will travel from the U.S. to Japan in four hours. Right now the trip between the two countries takes more than twice as long!

As the plane will travel faster than a bullet, its nose and wing edges will heat to temperatures hot enough to bake a cake. That's a problem for a plane – it will have to be made of metals that can take repeated heating and cooling without weakening. If a metal weakens, it can fracture.

There's another problem. An airplane that breaks the speed of sound, or a supersonic airplane, has to have a long, pointed nose. But it's difficult for pilots to see past the nose when they land and take off. The Concorde solves this problem with a nose that lifts and droops, but it's heavy. The new plane will have no front windows! Instead there will be a big display in the cockpit, showing what's ahead.

The possibilities for machines of the future are fascinating. Here is one unusual design for a futuristic space transporter. What do *you* think extreme machines will look like?

Space travel
Many people dream about space travel, and there are incredible plans for all sorts of spacecraft. Some of these ideas will never be more than models. Others may eventually take off!

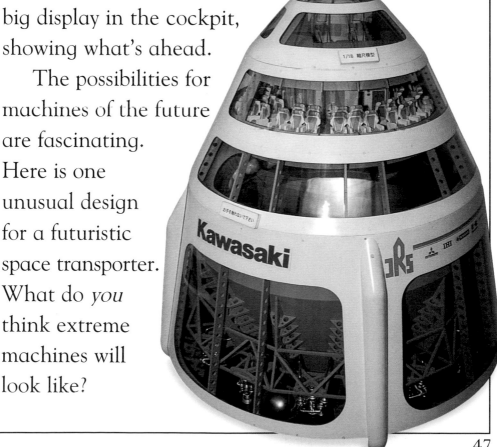

Glossary

Aerodynamic
The smooth, streamlined shape that helps a car or airplane to slip through air easily.

Circuit
A set course around which machines can race.

Drag racer
The name given to cars and motorbikes which race short distances (usually a quarter of a mile) in a straight line.

Endurance race
A race run over a long distance which takes a long time. Driving skill and a reliable engine are more important than speed.

Fuel
The material that powers an engine to make it go.

Gears
These control the speed of an engine.

Glider
Any airplane that doesn't have an engine to drive it is a glider. When the space shuttle runs out of fuel to power its engine, it becomes a glider. It glides back down to Earth.

Grandstand
A seating area for a crowd watching a sporting event.

Horsepower
A means of measuring an engine's power.

Hull
The part of a boat that sits in the water.

Hydroplane
A fast motorboat that skims over the water with most of its hull in the air. At speed the flat shape of the hull planes across the surface, rather than cutting through the water. Hydroplanes are the fastest racing boats.

Jet engine
All engines run on two things: fuel and oxygen. Jet engines gulp their oxygen from air.

Land speed record
The fastest speed set by a vehicle on land. The record has been broken many times. It is now faster than the speed of sound.

Rocket engine
A rocket engine carries the oxygen it needs in a tank in a special substance called an oxidizer. See also **Jet engine**.

Rotor
The whirling blades above a helicopter are known as rotors because of the way they spin. Each rotor is a mini-wing that lifts as it rotates.

Shock wave
Anything going faster than the speed of sound creates a shock wave in the air. We hear it as a loud bang. It can shatter glass at close range. If you could see it, it would look a bit like the bow wave that big, fast-moving ships create.

Space shuttle
The space shuttle is made up of an orbiter, two booster rockets, and a fuel tank. The orbiter can return to space again and again.

Speed of sound
Sound moves very much slower than light – that's why you see lightning before you hear it. At ground level where air is thickest, sound travels at about 760 mph.

Submersible
A submarine cruises underwater as well as diving and climbing. A submersible mainly just dives and climbs. Submersibles are carried to a new site by a mother ship and then lowered over the side.

Throttle
The control handle or pedal that feeds fuel to an engine. As it is opened, more fuel is pumped in and the engine speeds up. To slow down, the throttle has to be closed.